MICHELLE'S BOOK

by Anne Rothman and Kenneth Hicks

Illustrated by Lynn Adams

A Banbury Book

Published by
Banbury Books, Inc.
353 West Lancaster Avenue
Wayne, Pennsylvania 19087

ISBN: 0-88693-092-8
First printing — August 1984
6   5   4   3   2   1
Printed in the United States of America

This book is for

Michelle, Michaela, Michal, Michaelina, Micheline,
Mickie, Michelina, Micaela, Mikaela, Michaeline,
Michel, Michaella and Michele

In a time that you can't remember, before you were born, your parents had a big decision to make. They had to figure out which name to give you.

Because it was such a big decision, they thought about it a long, long time. They whispered names back and forth to each other. They wrote lists of names on pieces of paper. They looked in books. They thought and thought.

Then, someone said the name Michelle, and that was it! Michelle was just right.

Did you ever wonder why they picked that name?

Maybe your parents called you Michelle because someone they liked very much also had that name. An aunt. A grandmother. A friend.

Maybe your parents called you Michelle because it is such a popular name. In fact, it is used in many countries around the world. If you lived in Germany, your name might be Michaeline. In Italy, your name would be Michaella or Michaele. In France, it would be the same as it is now, Michelle. Or, it could be spelled Michel.

In England, there are many pretty ways to say and spell Michelle. Little girls are called Michaela, Micheline and Michaelina. Sometimes, they are called Mickie as a pet name. However it's spelled, Michelle is a lovely name.

Maybe your parents gave you that name because they knew its secret meaning. According to the Bible, the angel Michael guarded over the nation of Israel. He was the leader of all God's angels in the war against Satan and his evil band. During his great fight against Satan, Michael's battle cry rang through the heavens—"Who is like God?" That is what Michelle means in the Hebrew language.

Today, the feast of the angel Michael is celebrated on September 29th. It is called Michaelmas Day. In England, there is a custom that if you eat goose on Michaelmas Day you will have plenty of money for a year.

In Ireland, finding a ring in the Michaelmas pie meant that you would have an early marriage.

There is a flower which blooms in September or October around the feast day. It is called the Michaelmas daisy. Some people call it the heath daisy because it grows wild on the grassy heaths in England.

Another nice plant is Michelia, an evergreen. Originally, it grew only in China. Travelers to China loved the Michelia so much that they brought it home. The flowers have a scent like bananas. They are yellowish white with maroon edges.

In ancient times, according to legend, the angel Michael appeared to people on Earth. Probably the best-known appearance was at a place in France called Mont-Saint-Michel.

Mont-Saint-Michel is a small mountain of granite off the coast of Normandy. At low tide, it is surrounded by sandbanks which can be crossed on foot. But twice a day the tide comes rushing in and the mountain becomes an island.

The island and town are named after the angel Michael. Tradition says that Michael was seen on the island, dressed in a flowing gown of purest white with outstretched sword glistening in the sun.

Maybe your parents named you after someone else well-known in history and hoped you would grow up to be just like her. Michelle has been very popular as a girl's name for a long time.

One of the earliest and most famous Michelles was the daughter of Saul, the first King of Israel. Her name was spelled Michal.

Michal was the youngest daughter of Saul and the prettiest.

After David killed the giant Goliath, he fell in love with her. But David was only the poor son of a sheep herder and still very young himself. In order to marry the King's daughter, he had to prove his ability to take care of her.

Saul said that David would prove his worthiness if he could defeat one hundred of the enemy in battle. If David returned with one hundred belts, Saul said, he was worthy of marrying Michal.

David welcomed the challenge. Because he loved Michal, and she was so beautiful, he killed two hundred of the enemy. When he brought back two hundred belts, he was married to Michal with the full blessing of Saul.

Later, David became a great warrior in Saul's army. He won many battles and the people admired him.

They called his name as he passed by. Children ran after him through the streets. Though Michal was proud of him, her father, Saul, became jealous.

One night, Saul sent men to David and Michal's house. He told the men to stand watch and to kill David when he came out in the morning. Michal learned of the plot and helped David escape. Then she put a carving of David's head and a pillow of goat's hair in David's bed. She arranged the covers carefully and told her father's men that David was sick.

The next day, Saul's men sneaked up on the bed and tried to stab David with their long, sharp knives. But all they hit was the goat's hair pillow. Michal had tricked them and David was safe in the countryside.

There are many famous Michelles in modern times. Michelle Mouton is a race car driver. Racing cars is an extremely dangerous sport. The cars go very fast around sharp turns, and there are many accidents.

Almost all race car drivers have been men. But Michelle is an outstanding driver who has proven her skill racing against many men. In 1981, she won the San Remo Rally, becoming the first woman to ever win a world championship race.

Michelle Morgan, a French woman, is well-known for the things she has done to help children in need. She was awarded the Ceres Medal by the United Nations. The French have honored her by making a coin with her picture on it.

Micheline Oestermyer is a famous athlete who took part in the Olympic Games. In the Olympics, the best athletes from every country come together and compete for prizes. Micheline won a gold medal in 1948 in the games held in London, England. Her event was throwing the shot-put, a big ball of steel that weighs twelve pounds.

Some Michelles are in show business.

Michelle Pfeiffer is a movie actress. Michael Learned is a television and movie star. She is best known as the mother on the television show "The Waltons." That was one of the most popular TV shows ever made.

Michala Petri, from Denmark, plays a musical instrument called the recorder. She was a big success at the Mostly Mozart Festival in New York in 1983. The newspapers called her the "hit of the festival."

Michelle is also used in songs and poems because the name makes a pleasant rhyme. The Beatles, a singing group, wrote a song called "Michelle." It started off with the words, "Michelle ma belle," which means "Michelle my beautiful one" in French.

Here is a funny little poem about a girl named Michelle:

There once was a girl named Michelle,
Who liked a musician quite well.
    She joined his brass band,
    Which was touring the land,
'Cause her voice was as clear as a bell.

These are only a few of the people who have been named Michelle. As you grow older, you are sure to learn about many more. Who knows, maybe someday another little girl will be named just for you.